D0453730

"Think Like a Donor engages the reader through pithy truisms that have the added benefit of being inspirational. It's fun simply to read through and easy to understand with a lot of unplanned smiles of recognition, for it's not always the newness of information that gets into our minds – it's the reminder through a different prism."

> – **Doug White**, author of *The Art of Planned Giving*
> and *Charity on Trial*

"Our clients have enjoyed Wayne Olson's wit and wisdom over the years. His new book is packed with creative ideas that will motivate your donors."

> – **Ardis Schultz**, Executive Vice President,
> Crescendo Interactive

"There's something for everybody in this quick read, both reminders and new ideas. Spend a few minutes with Wayne Olson's interesting book and increase your fundraising by thousands of dollars."

> – **E.S.S.**, Donor

"Anyone who has heard Wayne speak knows the sad part: his presentation eventually has to end. Now you can have some of his best advice right at your fingertips. There is something for everyone in this wonderful edition!"

> – **Jeff Fulgham**, Development Director,
> National D-day Memorial Foundation

"When Wayne Olson speaks, I and many others in the nonprofit world listen. Wayne has a knack for giving common sense advice in brief and memorable ways. He is sharing a wealth of experience in this book, and it will be a valuable tool for fundraising professionals for years to come."
>   – **Brydon DeWitt**, President, Dewitt & Associates

"Wayne Olson's collection of fundraising principals and practices provides us with unique insight into the human dynamics of donor relations and professional integrity. If 'activity, knowledge, know-how, and inspiration to action' are the keys to success, as W. Clement Stone claims, you now hold in your hands the keys to successful fundraising and the art of teaching the joy of giving."
>   – **J. Herb Bailey, CFRE**, Director of Planned Giving, University of North Carolina Wilmington

"Cover to cover wisdom. This book will not only improve your donor relations, it will improve all of your relations. Implement Wayne's wisdom today."
>   – **David Webb**, TV Producer

"Wayne Olson's approach to fundraising is refreshingly human."
>   – **Pat Germelman**, Development Director, Fan Free Clinic

"What Wayne says is something we as fundraisers have always heard. However, he puts it in terms that are easy to understand, remember and implement."
>   – **Harold L. West, CFRE, FLMI**, Senior Director of Gift Planning, Meredith College

Think Like a Donor

Edited by Nancy Jones
Cover concept by Heather Olson
Cover designed by Katie Casler, Casler-design.com
Printed in the United States of America

ISBN 978-0-578-02722-7

THINK

Like A Donor

Creative & Simple Ideas for Getting
More Gifts & Improving Donor Relations

Wayne Olson

White Trout Press | Richmond, Virginia

Contents

Think Like a Donor

Introduction

You may remember a scene in the movie, *Doc Hollywood*, where Dr. Ben Stone, played by Michael J. Fox, walks beside a lake.

In the middle of the lake, two local men fish from a boat. One of them, Mr. McClory, had visited the doctor in an earlier scene, where Doc Hollywood had removed a fishing hook from his finger.

When the Fox character sees McClory in the boat, he shouts across the water warning him to be careful. McClory playfully responds, "We're not using hooks today!"

Moments later, a column of water shoots from the depths of the lake a few yards from the boat. Doc Stone, still walking along the bank, is stunned by the explosion.

The men were fishing with dynamite.

Presumably, the fishermen believed a good explosion would incapacitate the fish and they would float to the surface either dead or dazed for easy harvesting.

Fundraising's a lot like that classic scene from *Doc Hollywood*. Somewhere along the line, we all get a hook in the finger. It hurts.

We look for ways to fish without hooks. We turn to dynamite. We see our friends fishing with the magic sticks in the lake next door and wonder why we should not do the same. However, fundraising is not like dynamite. Fundraising, *true* fundraising, is about patience and the most basic of skills: relationship-building.

This book explores simple ideas donors like: What makes people want to give to a cause? Contrary to commonly accepted wisdom, a fundraiser, even a skilled one, can never give the donor a reason to give. Either the donor has a passion for the mission or the donor does not.

Good fundraisers identify the donor's passion, nurture it and then reward it.

In a deliberate, practical sense, this book shows how to fan those flames of passion, fuel compassion for your group's mission and shed light on ways you can help the donor make a gift. Enjoy reading these pages, and look for ways to encourage potential donors to feel even more like giving to your organization.

To

Heather,

Nathan and Mark

My thanks and heartfelt gratitude to Granddad, Ardis, Charles, Dick, Bob, Johnny, Forest, Tom and Rob, who taught me the enduring values of integrity and of a story well told.

The Power of a Story

Marketing Makeover

There are numerous billboards in my town advertising two hospitals that compete for business.

One hospital's campaign highlights the fact that if you go to its emergency room, you will be seen in thirty minutes or less. It does not advertise the competency of the doctors and staff, or excellence of its equipment.

Donors are not always looking for what we think. Advertise and tailor all messages, big and small, to what gets the donor's attention and motivates a completed gift. The doctors at one hospital may be better than the other, but if patients aren't coming to the emergency room, the entire hospital suffers.

The Value of a Man

"Never respect men merely for their riches, but rather for their philanthropy; we do not value the sun for its height, but for its use."

– Gamaliel Bailey

Little Is Big

My wife loves art festivals. I usually admire the eye-catching paintings or sculptures. She is quick to remind me that the big, grandiose pieces may have starving artists behind them.

She says to look at what is selling: corkscrews, sugar bowls and other pieces of smaller art. While most people cannot afford the expensive, large pieces at such a festival, they still want to bring *art* home. They may look at the large ones, but they buy the small ones.

While the salt shaker maker may not win any prizes or ribbons, he may have the largest savings account. What small things or services do we consistently offer to our constituents to encourage all sizes of gifts? Many small gifts can add up to propel a big mission.

We Are What We Do

The best stories are told with action and movement. Donors give to *what we do* and not to our name or our history.

When reaching out to donors, we raise more funds by telling and showing donors what we are doing and what we will do together, rather than who we are. Again, donors give to action, not names. Who we are is best told with verbs, not nouns and adjectives. When writing a letter, invitation or appeal, make sure it contains plenty of action.

Naming Names

When Walt Disney created Disneyland, he insisted that his employees were part of a *show*. Accordingly, people who work for Disney are *cast members* and not employees.

Even the ones we never see are cast members; they are just *backstage*.

Do our donors want to be called *prospects* or something else? There is not a good word for a future donor that sounds simple and authentic. The person who creates such a phrase will raise more funds. What do we call our future donors? For that matter, are we *fundraisers* or are we something else?

The Glamour of Unglamorous Duty

Always be prepared – even seek out – unglamorous duty. Everyone has to take out the trash from time to time. At Busch Gardens, every supervisor at every level must carry a broom when walking through the park.

Everyone should do everything for the mission – and be seen as willing to do so. Donors notice. Donors respond. If we are too good to do certain tasks, donors may find their dollars are too good to give.

Getting Our Ducks in a Row

The Peabody Hotel in Memphis is among the best in the world. It has a superior reputation for excellence and luxury. But it has something else: ducks.

The ducks are paraded to and from the lobby's fountain where they leisurely swim all day. Guests love the hotel's luxury, but they *remember* the ducks. What traditions or heritage do we have that we can highlight? Hotels should not have ducks. However, one very successful one does.

What is it we do that sets us apart? Find and highlight it and people will spread the word about your organization the same way they talk about the Peabody's famous ducks.

Ghost Stories

Have you noticed that so many bed and breakfasts have ghost stories about their places? Their websites and literature often boasts tales of the *permanent residents*. Why? In a world where even the most luxurious bed and breakfast can be indistinguishable from any other, there is a need to be memorable. There is a need to be set apart.

What better way than with a ghost story? It gives the bed and breakfast character and gives the guests something to talk about. While we may not have ghostly tales, what stories can we tell? What does your organization have that no one else does? Tell *that* story.

Be Swift to Tell the Story

Everyone likes a good story. Since cave people first scribbled stick figures on walls, we have told and listened to stories.

People *want* to hear the story about what your organization has accomplished and what it will accomplish. Use concise and specific examples. Keep your eyes and ears open for situations that would make a good story. However, *story* does not mean *fable*. Give your donor a story he or she can relate to and the gifts will follow. That gift often makes a great story for the next donor!

An Attitude of Gratitude

Clocking In

Whether you are meeting one donor or giving a presentation to thousands of listeners, never say, "I am running low on time."

That phrase and others like it convey a sense that we are not prepared and did not anticipate all we had to do or cover. It adds nothing. If you need to indicate to the donor or audience that time is short, say, "In the interest of *your* busy schedule, I'll wrap things up." Never run low on time. Portray preparedness and confidence.

Make It Easy to Reach You

Is your cell phone number on your business card? Your competitors' cards likely contain a cell number. Which card is more valuable to the donor?

Charity Begins at Home, but Does Not End There

Volunteer and give to other charities, not just your own.

The experience is guaranteed to show another viewpoint: that of the volunteer or donor. By placing yourself in the role of the donor, you see your organization in new, helpful ways.

Approachable People Make Donations Possible

People give to people.

People may be passionate about causes, missions and charities, but they give only to people. Make sure you are the kind of person to whom other people want to give.

If you have not read Dale Carnegie's classic, *How to Win Friends and Influence People*, it is well worth reading. Its message will help you become more approachable; and help you become one who people want to give more to.

Be Realistic

"Do a few things well rather than a lot of things poorly." – Wayne Olson

Master Your Schedule

Slow and steady wins the race. Resist giving in to the temptation to be an overachiever. Rest. Take it easy.

With a realistic schedule, it is easier to master the basics. Be on time. Do not over-schedule your day.

Arriving late, tired, or distracted when visiting a donor sends the message that our previous meeting, next meeting or something else is more important than the donor.

Handwritten is Well Written

In this age of text messages and email, your personal communication stands out.

A handwritten note including the words *thank you* will go a very long way, be fondly remembered, and will most likely be saved.

Own Errors Before They Own you

Embrace errors. Mistakes and oversights are chances for you to show your constituent your true level of devotion, and that you are human.

Think about the last time you tried to return something to a store and heard, "No, we do not accept returns." Where are you more likely to shop next time? There, or the store that cheerfully refunded your money with no questions asked?

Listen with New Ears

Empathy is not just about walking in another's shoes; first you must remove your own shoes. – Indian proverb

Count Appearance; Appearance Counts

The most successful corporations pay careful attention to each employee's appearance.

Rules commonly include no sitting, eating or even leaning on duty. The idea is to show customers respect and that employees are ready to serve. Appearance may not have much to do with performance, but donors will perceive that it does.

Be Seen

Freely hand out clothing with your logo on it to employees and volunteers. Allow employees to attend ALL your events, especially if they are wearing your *uniforms*.

Consumers pay more to wear less worthy logos. Some corporations and Fifth Avenue retail icons contribute far less to society than your organization does as a nonprofit. Why not raise your corporate or charitable logos to the same level?

Put your clothing where your mission is. Put your mission where your clothing is.

Kindness

My grandfather, Lester Olson, was a successful Tampa businessman. I asked him the secret for longevity and how he grew his business and treated customers.

He always said, "Kill them with kindness." When we shower our donors, volunteers and staff with kindness, our fundraising needs take care of themselves – really. The advice is simple, but carrying it out can be difficult.

You Are the Difference

To donors, YOU are the charity. YOU are the mission. Every day, remember that if your mission was a living, breathing person, it would look like you, sound like you, and think like you. You are the mission and the organization. It does not exist without *you*.

Make Giving Easy

The Only Way to Ask

Asking for money does not often work – unless you are a whining teenager or child asking a parent – and even then it is not a sure thing.

People do not like to give money.

They want to partner with you so they can accomplish common goals *with* you. Even the most passive donors see a gift as an investment in a common cause.

Do not ask for a donation.

Ask the donor to partner with you and allow you to work for the donor's interests by mobilizing the resources and infrastructure of your organization. Offer to work for the donor, rather than asking the donor to work for you.

To Build a Ship

"If you want to build a ship, don't drum up the men to gather wood, divide the work and give orders. Instead, teach them to yearn for the vast and endless sea." – Antoine de Saint-Exupery

Voice Mail that Shouts

Be different. It seems almost everyone is on the other line or away from his or her desk.

Let your voice mail message be another motivator for your cause. Each week, tell donors a new fact about your mission. Rather than being away from your desk, be "meeting with donors who want to help you build the new Regional Science Center," or "learning about the latest tax laws to assist our valued donors."

Of course, your own friendly voice is better than voice mail, so answer calls promptly. Include your cell phone number in your message so donors can reach you.

More Lanes Handle More Traffic

Want more traffic in your donations? Give donors more lanes. Expand your web presence and make sure your website makes it easy to give. Accept credit cards, payroll deduction and PayPal.

Remind your donors of websites where retailers donate a portion of each sale to the consumer's favorite causes. Even on the most basic level, have a donation box right in your office or nearby where people can easily give and be reminded of the importance of giving.

There is a megachurch in Longwood, Florida that no longer passes the offering plate. It places boxes near the doors where people can give when they feel like it. Other charities allow donors to give by automatically withdrawing an agreed amount from donors' checking accounts each month.

Use the Internet Wisely

Make your website name and email address easy to find.

There is no rule that says a website name has to be some variation of that organization's name. Certainly have that one, but also use a simple, memorable name that points to your content. That way, donors can locate it without confusion. For example, *wayneo.com* is better than *woenterprisesinc.com*. *Happydonor.com* is even better.

Email addresses are the same. You would not let your IT department dictate the name on your nametag, your street address or company name. Your website and email address are no less important. Use an email address that is easy to remember and helps donors contact you.

Driving Miss Donation

Appearances can be deceiving. If we ask what brand sells the most cars in the United States, the response would probably be Toyota, Ford or Honda. None are even close to being the true biggest seller.

According to toy maker Mattel's website, Hot Wheels brand has sold more than four billion cars since 1968 – more than the sales of Chrysler, Ford and General Motors combined.

When you ask which donors have the most to give, sometimes the answer is not what it might seem. Think outside the box – or in this case, outside Detroit or Japan – for the correct answer.

Eyes Can Deceive You

Never judge someone's ability to give by what he or she wears, what he or she drives, or where he or she lives.

Donors living in a modest home without a mortgage often have more money than those living in upscale neighborhoods and driving luxury cars with big payments.

Debtors' Prison

People rarely give to help a charity get out of debt. Don't ask.

If a nonprofit organization is in debt, it is often better to ask top donors not to *give*, but to help figure a way out of debt. They may give anyway, and they will be impressed that your forward thinking reminds them of the way they earned their money.

The Most Important Fundraiser

Does your receptionist know he or she is a prominent fundraiser and your organization's Director of First Impressions?

As a teenager, I worked with the parking lot team at Busch Gardens. Supervisors told us we were the most important employees in the park. They were right. We made the first and last impression on each guest.

When donors contact a charity, the people who answer the phone, open the door or seat guests are your number one impression makers. Do they know how important they are?

Manners Matter

"Good manners will open doors that the best education cannot." – United States Supreme Court Justice Clarence Thomas.

Passion Power

People give passionately.

From a charity's point of view, a donation is generally a financial transaction. From the donor's, it is almost purely emotional.

Whether asking for volunteers or hiring staff, we should hire passion and train expertise, rather than trying to hire experts and train them to be passionate for the cause.

Location, Location, Donation

Retailers know the placement of cereal on a shelf or a sign's location at a gas station can make a big difference in sales.

What wonderful tools are already on our shelves that just need to be moved to eye level? We may not need to create new ideas, but merely move existing ones into better light.

An Encouraging World

Reward employees with your resources. Walt Disney World hosts a number of events at the park for its employees during off-hours.

The Company gives cast members previews of new attractions and allows them to compete in canoe races around the Rivers of America. They feel special and the company is gladly sharing existing resources that are readily available.

Numerous studies show people are more inspired by kindness than by money. What resources can you share with employees that costs little, but energizes them to do more?

Handbooks Help

Have a handbook that outlines every procedure. Use it. Stick to it.

Respect this valuable tool and so will your employees and donors. Using a handbook demonstrates consistency and clearly shows your intent to be here in the future. Include an Investment Policy Statement and Gift Acceptance Policy. These are great resources. Freely share both policies with donors, and they will share gifts with you.

Stamp It

For a few cents more than regular postage, you can put your own picture on a United States postage stamp. What if a sponsor or a special donor received an invitation or thank you with his or her picture on it? Check out stamps.com for information about their services. You are limited only by your imagination and your budget.

Stamp It – Part II

Donors are inundated with mail that looks alike. Make your envelopes stand out. The post office sells stamps in many designs, shapes and sizes. Your letter has a better chance of being opened when the donor notices it. A colorful, eye-catching stamp costs no more than a common one, but can lead to uncommon results.

Stamp It – Part III

Make personal notes more *personal* by avoiding the postage meter whenever possible. Opt for stamps instead.

To the donor, every gift is personal. Look for ways to be personal whether we are asking for support or thanking the donor.

The Power is in You

This Little Light of Mine

"Catch on fire with enthusiasm and people will come for miles to watch you burn."

– John Wesley

Promises, Promises

We should not say anything to donors we do not mean. Keep all promises, no matter how big or small. I once passed an acquaintance at a convention and told him I would call him the next day. I did.

To this day he regards me as a man of my word. Not for any grand gesture, but because I simply called him as I said I would.

We never know what promises a donor will consider important. If we limit our promises to only those we will keep, the difference does not matter.

Dating for Dollars

Fundraising is a lot like marriage. Traditionally, when a man proposes marriage, he generally knows the answer. Her response does not depend on the way the question is asked. It is how the couple developed their relationship that counts.

If you have developed your relationships with donors correctly, you will know what the answer to the question will be. The way you ask the question has little influence over the answer. Yet in fundraising, many concentrate on the "ask" part of the question. So much so, the word "ask" has been corrupted from a verb to a noun.

One thing we can learn from a marriage proposal is to do it creatively, with the emphasis on the ultimate goal which is a long-lasting relationship.

Wants and Needs

What a charity needs is not necessarily what a donor wants to give.

People will want to contribute what they want to contribute. That does not always equal what the charity needs.

Adjust perspective from what the charity needs to what the donor might want to do. When you ask for money, aim high. Donors often comment they would have given more, but the charity asked for less; so they figured that's all the organization needed.

Helping Donors Helps You

We always benefit when we look out for the donor, even when helping the donor seems to mean not looking out for ourselves.

When a donor needs help making a gift to another charity, help the donor make it happen. The donor will often be so impressed you helped him that he will almost always help you.

Smile

"A smile is the shortest distance between two people." – Victor Borge

Never Shop on an Empty Stomach

The last day of the month, year or your fiscal year is not the time to call donors to ask for money – even if they gave at that time last year.

Just as we should never go to the grocery store on an empty stomach, we should never go to a donor to conduct business when we are up against an internal deadline or goal.

The need to meet a goal is powerful and can overwhelm better judgment.

Mouse House Rules

"You know what people want and you build it for them." – Walt Disney

Effortless Fundraising

When a donor includes a charity in his or her will, the gift is often in the tens of thousands of dollars. These gifts consistently come from people who lead humble lifestyles.

Only a small fraction of Americans include a charity in their will. Most say they didn't because they never thought about it.

Include language in all your publications and at the bottom of stationery, reminding donors to include your cause in their estate plans.

When in Touch, Be Out of Touch

Today, cell phones are everywhere. However, remember we control *them*. They do not control *us*.

When we answer our phone while meeting a donor, we have told the donor that no matter who calls, that person is more important than the donor. If an expected call is that crucial it is better to postpone the appointment to take that call. Otherwise, leave the phone in the car or turn it off.

Timing Is Everything

Donors want to feel important.

Feed this desire by always arriving early for appointments. Donors, especially older donors, value punctuality and will value you and your organization more when you arrive on time or early.

Mission First, but Not Always

Remember donors have lives outside of our missions. They will respect you and your efforts if sometimes the mission takes a back seat to life. While we may eat, sleep and breathe our mission and are exposed to it every day, even the most ardent volunteer or donor does not.

We are only a part of their lives – even if it is a big part. Everyone has competing interests for their time, devotion and money. Act accordingly.

Who's on First?

In theme parks, airlines and other industries, the most basic rule is "safety first." Every decision is weighed based on its impact on safety. While we should always be safety conscious no matter what, our rule is "donors first."

If we are not already thinking of donors first, we should be. It is worthy of being engraved and placed on a plaque over our office doors so we are reminded of it every time we venture out into the world.

Whose Campaign Is It?

With few exceptions, campaigns are created from the institution's point of view. Unless a campaign is for a limited purpose such as repairing the roof on a building, then it was likely created by a committee based on wants, not needs.

Wants are never as important as needs. Donors know this.

Never treat a campaign as do or die. Treat it with enthusiasm or energy, but know that donors will not relate to any sense that the campaign is everything – unless it really is. Artificial urgency results in real disappointment.

Forbidden Words

Veteran broadcasters train themselves to never use words they would not use on the air. When proper language is a habit, there is less chance the wrong word might be said on the air.

Similarly, we should never describe a donor in terms we would not use in front of the donor. I once witnessed a fundraiser with his back to the door, describe how he should *hit up* a certain donor to help get a campaign going, because that donor was a *sucker* for gifts.

What he did not know was that the loyal donor had stopped by for a visit and was standing right behind him. It is not uncommon to run into donors in grocery stores, parks or around town. Always be prepared and assume the person next to you in traffic is someone you know.

Trust the Family First

Consider the charitable remainder unitrust. It is so named because the family receives benefits for a time, then whatever *remains* goes to charity.

While *remainder trust* is the official IRS designation, why not call it what it really is – a *family first trust*? It provides benefits to the family first and then benefits the charity later.

Consider what areas are routinely described from the charity's point of view that could be made more attractive by highlighting benefits to the donor.

Think Like a Donor

Thanks and Giving

Diet Rite Got It Right

At a large trade show Diet Rite Cola was giving away samples of its then, newly reformulated soft drink.

After the convention the drink company had dozens of cases left. I approached them and asked if they could donate some of the cases to our cause. They did. Then, as each of our clients (who were cancer patients and their families) later enjoyed a donated soda, we asked them to sign their names using one of the colorful pens we left next to a large thank you note. We later presented the note to the supervisors of the thoughtful people at Diet Rite who were responsible for the gift.

Our clients received a refreshing drink, the Diet Rite representatives did not have to make arrangements to ship back the extra cases, and their supervisors knew what good employees they had. Everyone benefited. Are there any companies or vendors near you who can offer something that presents a similar, simple solution where everyone benefits?

Listen and You Will Receive

Just listening to people is a gift to them. In our world few people take time to listen to others and when they do, it is usually not for long.

The world has enough bloggers. We need more listeners. Donors appreciate people who can simply pay attention. There are many talented gift officers who can spend hours with a donor and say only a couple words. Be one of them.

When You Don't Know What to Do

Ask your donors for advice.

If you want an appointment, ask a donor if you could see him or her and ask for advice. Keep your word and do not solicit or accept a donation.

Great questions include, "What can I do to raise more money for our cause from people you know?" or, "What is the best way to honor you or people like you for your accomplishments?"

There is no better way to honor a donor and get the appointment, than to ask for advice. Remember, too, the adage that never fails: "If you want advice, ask for money. If you want money, ask for advice."

Thank Donors Freely

As construction on Walt Disney World was ending, Bub Thomas and other entertainers performed for the construction workers to show their appreciation for building the theme park.

The construction workers and their families received a priceless gift. The performers got to fine-tune their acts and feel genuine appreciation. Look for ways to thank donors and clients that are meaningful, yet priceless.

The Only Answer to True Trouble

When you call a business to complain, what do you usually hear? Often the answer is a version of "Too bad, because that's our policy." You, as a customer, deserve better.

Donors may call you to complain and they expect to hear a rehearsed response outlining corporate policy or making excuses. Turn foes to friends instead, by offering a sympathetic ear and a promise to do better next time. The best answer is one that identifies with the donor. "That's horrible," is the only answer the donor wants to hear and is often the only answer you should give.

When something goes wrong, admit the mistake so you can immediately set out to correct it.

Treat Money Like Donors Do

Be frugal. Donors will give us more money when they have confidence that a charity respects their funds the way they do.

Personally use money-saving offers such as coupons, priceline.com, hotwire.com, and let your donors know you do.

Naming Names

Dale Carnegie said, *"...a man's name is to him the sweetest and most important sound in any language."*

When we remember and use people's names, we sing their song. When we remember the names of their children, friends and pets, we conduct a symphony!

Capture the Moment

Anyone can buy an affordable digital camera that takes excellent photographs. Buy one and keep it with you. Any opportunity to take a photo of a donor, the donor's pets, or donor's garden is an opportunity to build a relationship. The photos cost little, but the moments they capture are priceless.

The author poses with legendary
radio personality, Harvey Hudson

Give Donors a Piece of Your Organization

The University of Richmond is a beautiful campus with a lush landscape filled with beautiful trees. When I worked for the University we had the idea of cutting down a tree and making picture frames and thanking donors with them.

We could never get permission or the money to cut down a tree. Then a massive hurricane blew through Virginia and the campus was littered with fallen trees. We had a local craftsman make frames from the free wood for less cost than many off-the-shelf gifts. The hand-crafted frames were gorgeous, appreciated, and unique.

Hold on to creative ideas. You never know when the impossible can become possible. Good things can come from bad hurricanes.

Actions Make the Best Words

What we say is not nearly as important as what we do. I once was searching for words to describe Bub Thomas, a gifted musician, talented artist and beloved friend, who worked at Walt Disney World.

Even when Bub was well into his eighties, he still took the stairway two steps at a time to get to his second floor office. No words could adequately describe his love and enthusiasm for this job and genuine affection for the people he worked for and with. Anyone seeing him bound up the steps would immediately see the authenticity of the man.

Take the steps two at a time. Donors will follow.

Reward Donors and They Will Reward You

Psychologists say we humans do not do what we are told to do. We do what we are rewarded for doing.

When we make donors feel appreciated for what they have already done, they will return to us again and again. Always look for ways to reward donors for giving. It could be a personal thank you, a small gift, or lunch together. Find ways to reward donors and they will reward you.

Thank Donors, Then Thank Them Again

A friend tells me you have not thanked a donor until you have thanked him or her seven times.

That does not mean each of the seven has to be said the same way, or in a grandiose manner. A sincere show of gratitude does more than offer appreciation for past actions – it sets the stage for future ones.

Thank donors seven times.

End With Fireworks

Many theme parks offer spectacular fireworks at the end of the day. Most park guests never stop to think why there are fireworks, other than they are beautiful or fun.

However, there is a more practical reason why theme parks end each day with a bang. Guests were leaving the parks during the heat of the day. If they leave, they are not buying drinks, t-shirts and other souvenirs. Nightly fireworks were scheduled to encourage guests to stay.

Give donors fireworks. Reward them with something spectacular, gorgeous and wondrous. They will appreciate the fireworks and donors will stay.

Think Like a Donor

Index

S

stamp, 56, 57
stamps.com, 56

T

Tampa, 39
theme parks, 72, 91
Thomas, Bub, 81, 88
Thomas, Hon. Clarence,
    51
Toyota, 47

U

University of Richmond,
    86

V

Victor Borge, 65

W

Walt Disney, 22, 67
Walt Disney World, 54,
    81
Wesley, John, 60

A Final Thought and an Invitation

What works for you? We are already busy preparing a new book on donor relations and fundraising – this time written by you!

The best ones will be published in our next book. Please send your submissions to:

wayne@thinklikeadonor.com

Most of all thank you for reading

Think Like a Donor!

Want to think more like a donor?

Wayne Olson is available to talk with your charity, church, group or organization. For speaking information or discounts on bulk orders of *Think Like a Donor*, please contact us at:

info@thinklikeadonor.com

or

wayne@happydonor.com

Personalize

Think Like a Donor

with your organization's name and logo.

We can economically add a personal introduction or gift page to your specifications and customize content so you can give your staff, board and volunteers copies of this book, as if they were printed by you! Let them know how important they are to you and how vital fundraising is to your organization.

For more information:

info@thinklikeadonor.com

or

wayne@happydonor.com

The author as an engineer on
Busch Gardens Engine No. 9, circa 1986.

About the Author

Wayne Olson is a frequent writer and speaker on fundraising, nonprofit marketing, and corporate and donor relations. His articles appear in *Planned Giving Today* and he is a regular contributor to Crescendo Interactive and GiftLegacy. He is president of the Virginia Gift Planning Council and teaches fundraising and donor relations at the University of Richmond.

Wayne has spoken to International AFP Conferences in Atlanta, Dallas and New Orleans, and to the Practical Planned Giving Conferences in Orlando, Chicago and San Diego.

Prior to his work as a fundraiser for the American Cancer Society and the University of Richmond, Wayne was a litigation attorney, specializing in corporate and contract law. Before law school Wayne was a journalist producing and anchoring television and radio news broadcasts. As a youth in Florida, Wayne worked in almost every operations position at Busch Gardens, Tampa. Despite his accomplishments writing, fundraising and as an attorney, Wayne's children still prefer to think of him as an engineer on the steam train at Busch Gardens.